Deception Island

Selected Earlier Poems 1974–1999

WILLIAM LOGAN has published eight books of poetry and five of essays and reviews. *The Undiscovered Country* won the National Book Critics Circle Award in Criticism. He teaches at the University of Florida and lives in Gainesville, Florida, and Cambridge, England.

Also by William Logan

POETRY
    Sad-faced Men (1982)
    Difficulty (1984, 1985)
    Sullen Weedy Lakes (1988)
    Vain Empires (1998)
    Night Battle (1999)
    Macbeth in Venice (2003)
    The Whispering Gallery (2005)
    Strange Flesh (2008)

CRITICISM
    All the Rage (1998)
    Reputations of the Tongue (1999)
    Desperate Measures (2002)
    The Undiscovered Country (2005)
    Our Savage Art (2009)

Deception Island

Selected Earlier Poems 1974–1999

William Logan

London

PUBLISHED BY SALT PUBLISHING
Dutch House, 307–308 High Holborn, London WC1V 7LL United Kingdom

All rights reserved

© William Logan, 2011

The right of William Logan to be identified as the
author of this work has been asserted by him in accordance
with Section 77 of the Copyright, Designs and Patents Act 1988.

This book is in copyright. Subject to statutory exception
and to provisions of relevant collective licensing agreements,
no reproduction of any part may take place without the written
permission of Salt Publishing.

Salt Publishing 2011

Printed and bound in the United Kingdom by Lightning Source UK Ltd

Typeset in Swift 9.5 / 13

*This book is sold subject to the conditions that it shall not,
by way of trade or otherwise, be lent, re-sold, hired out,
or otherwise circulated without the publisher's prior consent
in any form of binding or cover other than that in which
it is published and without a similar condition including this
condition being imposed on the subsequent purchaser.*

ISBN 978 1 84471 717 0 paperback

1 3 5 7 9 8 6 4 2

for Debora Greger

Contents

FROM *SAD-FACED MEN*	1
Deception Island	3
The Object	4
Observing Whales through Binoculars	6
Seventy-Six	7
Two Lives	9
Travel Report	11
Ice	12
The Man on the Bed	13
The Mantis	16
A Portrait by Bellocq	17
Tatiana Kalatschova	18
The Lizard in His Medium	20
FROM *DIFFICULTY*	21
Clare and Silence	23
Arcanum	24
The Angels among the Liars	26
Money and Dürer	27
Black Harbor	28
Summer Island	29
Blue Yacht	30
Travel	32
Folly	33
Green Island	34
The King of Black Pudding	35
Flour Mites as Moral Beings	36
This Island	37

FROM *SULLEN WEEDY LAKES*	39
Moorhen	41
Capability Brown in the Tropics	44
The Rivers of England	45
Banana Republics	46
Debora Sleeping	48
Christ Church, Oxford / 26 October 1881	50
3-13 September 1752	52
The Underground	53
Racial Prejudice in Imperial Rome	60
Major Graves	61
To the Honourable Committee	63
James at Sixty	65
Haddocks' Eyes	67
Ambassador of Imperfect Mood	69
FROM *VAIN EMPIRES*	71
The Secession of Science from Christian Europe	73
Christ among the Moneychangers, 1929	81
The Long Vacations	82
A Version of Pastoral	84
The Advent of Common Law in Littoral Pursuits	86
Florida Pest Control	88
The Shadow-Line	89
Van Gogh in the Pulpit	90
Britain without Baedeker	91
Tristes Tropiques	92
The Burning Man	93
Animal Actors on the English Stage after 1642	96
Flower, of Zimbabwe	97
Keats in India	98

FROM *NIGHT BATTLE*   107
    Florida in January   109
    Sundays in the South   110
    Mother on the St. Johns   112
    from Long Island Sins   113
    Blues for Penelope   115
    Nothing   116
    The English Light   118
    Larkin   119
    from Paradise Lost   120
    Song   122
    For the Hostages   123
    The Words   125
    Dear AC   126
    Dear DD   128
    My Father as Madame Butterfly   130
    Pera Palas   131
    Alexander Sarcophagus   132

Acknowledgments

Looking back over this quarter-century of work, I see the absences, the lost opportunities, the small gains. I have reprinted the poems almost as they were, though I could not resist some changes in attention or resolve or punctuation.

I am grateful to David Godine, who published *Sad-faced Men*, *Difficulty*, and *Sullen Weedy Lakes*, and to Penguin (US), which published *Vain Empires* and *Night Battle*. *Difficulty* was published in the UK by Salamander Press, and *Vain Empires* by Peterloo Poets.

Look, look, a mouse! Peace, peace;
this piece of toasted cheese will do't.

— KING LEAR

from *Sad-faced Men*

Deception Island

> *It provides an excellent harbor*
> *but occasionally the water boils.*
> — New York Times

A bird-like man waits
for the windows to clear. What will be there?
Natives dancing their unrepeatable dances.

A new species of tapir
wandering up from the valley. Perhaps only a river,
opal or indigo — on which black swans

hover as if at rest and at flight —
moving its mirror toward open sea.
A postcard shows a northern snow,

fur-coated men surrounding his clapboard house
where icicles lean on lines of light.
His coffee cools near an unfinished meal

in whose palette he finds unlikely attractions.
A tablecloth, a barren sky,
opens one blank horizon to another.

This is Antarctica. The bay in the drowned
volcano bubbles and dies.
The penguins waddle through ice

on their awkward feet. When the sun
reaches the top of the Spanish tower,
a parade of torches will begin,

each woman behind her blood-red mask.
She represents what blinds and what forgets,
the tropic sun that might rise anywhere.

The Object

Consider the tears
of a statue: made of wood, not water,
they neither swell nor move, but week
by week remain an object

of the steady, almost cruel
gaze of tourists. For such gazes, no tax
could suffice, as if a luxury tax
could justify such tears

or make stares less cruel.
Any lake, any body of water
makes us the object
of admiration, our own weak

tendencies expressed in the weak
reflection of light at dawn or sunset, a tax
on the eyes—we do not object,
though our eyes may tear

from long observation of the water
in which we find the cruel
transfiguration of cruel
Time, our adversary, and not a weak

one. From the clear water,
our earliest mirror, we first suffer attacks
of the spirit, those awful tears
in a pride whose object

is severed from subject, and object
found the lesser of the pair: a cruel
division, and crucial, as it tears
us away from ourselves. Weak

at first from such division, by further attacks
we grow weaker, and from the water
rise angered, calling the water
a betrayer, and the distance from the object

art: a length, an accounting, a tax
on imagination, which observes with cruel
compassion our alter ego, our weak
familiar shed wooden tears.

Observing Whales through Binoculars

Fountains in a gray field,
whales spout off the rough beach. A gray sky
meets the gray sea in a vague horizontal.
A black flipper scythes the water

beneath gulls scattered
through scarred lenses. No matter
that the wind registers on a ruptured sea.
The ear records a near soundless

tableau: only movements controlled
by the elements they move forth among.
Three blue phantoms watch from the white sand
and corn grass wavering

in a wavering air. Without binoculars,
we are diminished forms, figures
in a figurative scape. An orange-and-black dragger
cuts through the short waves. The sky is an irruption

of glamour into the material world.

Seventy-Six

Her dream rebuilt the packet ships, the port
no longer a port, the river silted
shallow, the gray light dead and wrong, tilted
east on the horizon. Failing moonlight
covers the wrinkled bed; the Fahrenheit
thermometer reads normal. She can go
home now. She clutches the portfolio
of her novel, unfinished yet. "I wrote
'The trout meander'—they don't. Do they? Your note
cheered me *immensely*. Of course the plot is bad—
no theme. Three boys must drown fishing. I had
two—your uncles. Boys, I mean. Jacksonville
is too warm for me. I prefer the hills
of Cohasset—you remember. Write soon.
The fish—of course! They slither." Afternoon,
a northern village, a northern river,
snow on the salt grass. The birds form over
Long Point. Their florid warning cries are feigned
or lost on air. She had been sick—it rained—
and during this pneumonia played Camille,
though not dying, not eating, getting well
with dramatic slowness. Writing in bed
made her weak and mad; to honor the dead,
her parents, depressed her. "This depression
makes me write," she wrote. "Voices in unison—
I hear them still—my parents, their old parents,
the cast-off Christian Scientists at Advent,
the whole believing lot. And now your success.
Your brothers will be rich—not you. Oh, yes.
Not you. The novel lengthens, lengthens, sits
like a wreck. Now I work on it in fits—
the climax is the storm of '98.
I cannot find the theme within the fate

of prose. But, please, no advice. I know where
the theme should be. In the pitch of weather—
when flooding took grandfather's property,
the river broke a new mouth to the sea."

Two Lives

I
JOSEPH CONRAD

Hypnotic moon on black water, floating
under a blank sky, no boat returning
to port tonight. Bodies in the water:
images that interrupt the calm life
in murderous England, where only wheat
moves like waves, or the rippling crowd of maids
where the anarchist lurks. Exile in the world,
he wrote these sure disasters out; they now
have barged into a world beneath the world,
where all hearts are bloody, all ignorance
certain as greed. In the uneasy light
at morning, we anxiously remember
the tall palms breaking in the midnight storm
or the convulsions of disease and love.

II

A Valentine for Matthew Arnold

The Seas of Faith are full again with vain
philosophies, empty orders of gods,
demons of the mind and heart converting
the slow angers of love to hollow stares
and rhetoric. These are not days to love,
when the rare expectations of morning
will be blackened by the shabby evening.
Let us be faithless to one another.
The monarch butterflies now copulate
in the kitchen, bats bare their teeth against
the screens, and throatless songbirds rasp all night.

At dawn, armies of toads and frogs litter
the walks. All animals act cruelly
toward each other. We are no different.

Travel Report

Just before dawn, when the crows practice
their four-noted alarm, sometimes managing
a brief chorus in unison, a last coolness
leaves the skin and heat moves in to stay.
Equipped with ceiling fans of indifferent
manufacture, the only hotel commands a view
of the gray dirt, coarse as salt, merging
unidentifiably with the yellow sky. At first
it seems a mistake to be here, and tourists
line up at the information office, demanding
explanations from a clerk who shrugs in sympathy.

Not even the guards care any longer
about immigrants who straggle over this country's
labyrinthine borders, but emigration is strictly
controlled by bribe. The indigenous lizards
dwell mostly underground and are losing
their keen sight and smell, their violent colors.
Under the old rulers, a pantheon of deities
was worshipped; but the real god is the sun,
hereditary and ubiquitous. By afternoon,
there is little to do except perfect the language,
spoken slowly and with difficulty.

This is a turned land, where people flee
from contact with each other and love, like plague,
is avoided. None of the residents is anxious to leave,
however; and tourists after a month or two
seem resigned to their location,
sinking into this country's welcoming languor.
The only road leads toward smaller, hotter countries.

Ice

Men are walking on the harbor!
Secure in the physics of temperature,
they step from boat to lodged boat.

under the fiery stars, cars play their headlights
over a white continent. The bay is a land of floes,
and every twelve hours the tides

lay up sheets of ice on the shore.
In a week, they are piled as high as a man,
a dozen strata, histories of the tidal night.

One morning, two days after warm weather,
the whole white shelf sinks into the sea,
leaving raw sand and the angry waves.

What has kept us from falling?
Not winter's weird equilibrium.
Or earth drawing the reluctant feet

down. Balance is the memory
of the fall, before it happens.
Our inner charts are navigators' guesses:

white floes, flaws, flyaway islands.
The stories that mapped Viking explorers.
Or Frobisher's five men, captured by Eskimo,

a tribe that three centuries after
remembered their release, the small boat
they built, the manner of their death.

Cold water, and England a long way.
We stay on land that holds us.
Or one morning walk out over the blue ice.

The Man on the Bed

My grandfather was no honest man,
for honesty is of little use to a man
who by profession sells kitchen gadgets
to people who will be hard-pressed recalling
the reason for their purchase. When I asked
how he persuaded Midwest housewives to buy
his merchandise, he said he often had luck
with an anecdote of one sort or another.
He then told me a story he had found
particularly good for such entertainment.
"Once," he would say to a stranger,
"when I was on a long sales-trip, my wife
was sick, I later discovered, with a cold
or the influenza, or a woman's complaint,
and was spending her days in bed. That evening,
clear for winter, she had retired early,
leaving the front door unlocked
for a neighbor who had promised to look in.
My wife fell asleep but sometime afterward
awoke feeling disturbed. She thought
it was snowing; yet through the oak branches
she could see the great full moon,
like a shining, whirling onion.
It cast a shaft of light across her bed,
the edges so sharp she reached to touch them.
Waving her hands in the moonlight,
she heard a double breath, her own breath
traveling into the room, through the light,
repeated. At first she was not alarmed—
or a-feared, as she would say.
She breathed, and heard the echoed breath.
She breathed more slowly; but each breath
was repeated just as slowly, so she could not tell
if she were hearing some other person breathe,
or if the sounds were just some trick of the ear,

as on a quiet day a voice just loud enough
will echo off the trees or houses near.
Beyond the moonlight, she saw a figure
on the edge of the bed. She thought at first
it was the neighbor woman, though at once
she knew this was a man. Convinced
I had come home early from my trip,
she sat up and called, 'Tike.'
The man on the bed did not speak.
She imagined I was daydreaming—or moonstruck!—
and had not heard her, so called the man
again by my name. He did not respond,
and my wife began to become uneasy.
She could not make out his features,
only his silhouette against the roses in the wallpaper.
She was too terrified to say another word,
too unnerved even to lie back on the pillow,
so remained there, sitting in the moonlight,
listening to them both breathe. At last the man
leaned toward her and said, in a very low voice,
'Don't worry. I will not hurt you.'
It was then that she began to scream.
Even now, she cannot remember what happened
after that. Later, she stopped screaming
and began crying; but the man was gone.
Too paralyzed to move, she cried until she slept.
It was morning when she awoke, yet hours
before she could force herself from the bed-clothes.
Wrapped in her robe, armed with a pair of scissors,
she opened the closets and stooped under tables,
ever afraid she would come upon him.
Now here is the strangeness of the matter.
My wife thought that, if not a woman raper,
the man might have been a burglar or a bum;
but nothing of value was missing, nor was there

less food in the icebox than the evening before.
When she came to the door, she found
that it was locked already. The door left open
was locked now from the inside. The poor girl
ran out to the neighbors' and refused to leave
until I returned some two weeks later.
Now I do not know whether to believe my wife,
who is by nature a nervous woman.
I'm inclined to think there was no strange man
on her bed—yet her fright was real enough.
She may have wanted me home so badly,
she dreamed that I was home, but, in the way
of dreams, did not answer when she called
my name. Or perhaps it was not me,
perhaps the man she dreamed of was Death.
I do not know." And slowly my grandfather
would add, "Or perhaps, and I think this
late at night, and the night clear and strange,
like that night, perhaps it was no dream,
perhaps Death himself sat upon her bed;
and she was so unstrung that he took pity
and decided to visit her some other night.
Now by daylight I'm as sane as you or anyone
and scarce credit that particular interpretation.
Still, I never leave her for too long now,
and for that reason," he would finish,
"might I interest you in the purchase
of one of these handy conveniences?"

The Mantis

Now prisoners of summer's air,
we admire the polluted sunsets
rising from Dulles. Two mantises
mate in the backyard holly,

thorned and wild. All one evening,
I return to watch their passion.
By morning the male has vanished—
eaten by his mate—

and the female disappears as I watch
sacs of spiders hatch in the neighbor's fir.
Days later, the mantis returns
to attack the window screen,

battering her head against the aluminum.
Like the children shouting all day
next door, I am fevered
by isolation. The closed backyards

circumnavigate a court
where spiders maneuver across the walls.
Monstrous crickets rub along
the living-room's mustard carpet:

There seems no way in. I let them go
outdoors by the rows of black
mailboxes. I find them again,
chewing grass seed in the metal shed,

thumping inside the plastic bags.
Tonight the airport lights
shake behind the cumulus. Inmates
of the basement are laying eggs for spring.

A Portrait by Bellocq

One day even this transfigured flesh will shatter
or burn, and its remains shower the dirt

where motions freeze in a simple light,
whether or not the season submits to death.

This light, not simple or singular, divides
the self from the self, the portion

that passes through it and moves beyond it
and lies down, and what is pictured forever,

drawn into visionary circumstance, a profile
against a shadowed door. How a submissive

meter infects the heart is difficult to explain.
Why is difficult to remember. In every woman,

there is a moment when the past precludes itself
from defeat or victory; and for you that moment

came when you left behind the shallow season
of the photographer and chose a future,

not of fire or decay, but one that would
lead there in its own slow fashion.

Tatiana Kalatschova

Only a woman of this measure
suits the industry model.
Among the headless torsos she stands,
unyielding and calm as a perfect

saint about to be burned. They sew
the cloth around her bones,
unlike anyone else's bones,
being noble, Russian, a measure

for all the dresses to be sewn
in her common size. When she models,
the designers become accustomed to the perfect
blonde posture her body takes as it stands

in their dresses. She understands
the satisfaction in bones
that year to year perfect
their proportions. Take her measure:

from it they have made mannequins, models
named for a dead czar's daughter, who sewed
as her sisters and servants sewed
rubies into pillows, then were made to stand

in the basement to be butchered by the model
soldiers who poured acid on their bones.
This Tatiana dances to a different measure,
the hem and drape of perfect

design. She need not perfect
the technique of the peasant, to sew
bolt and bolt of cloth without measure,
to harvest the corn when it stands,

to find in a chicken the bones
thin as the bones of a model.
But any woman, whether a model
to industry or blessed with imperfect

proportions, knows that skin will weaken her bones.
When the czar is murdered, let it not end so
quickly, she might say, unless she understands
that silence is itself a measure.

The Lizard in His Medium

Sly, like the French horn's plunge,
soft, like a child's whisper, the forked tongue
marks temperature, measures the wind's
currents. The tongue knows no true path.

The reptile's gentle lisp, his sinister
manners, his scale coat, his frangible tail:
what will he whisper when the lights go out?
How will he know our saurian taste?

"Hish-hish" washes over this. Was there
an eye more clear, more clever?
He has the leopard's hunger.
The flap ears close. He stalks and stalks.

He lives in observation of the moment's
flicker, the watched ascendancy of night:
it is the sharp minute in which he breathes.
To live beneath things supernal,

in that muted harmony that is eating and taking,
taking and giving back, his composition of pause,
where time is a weight and moment nothing.
The absent dark: his movement is silence.

The sand is only a temporary home.

from *Difficulty*

Clare and Silence

The grown faces men put on in their fits
are the fools of their imaginations.
The mad conscience this, the mad

delegate that, the mad live a mirror life,
hovering between the lark's
light exhaustion and the mortar of language.

We are the fashion of our dressy attitudes.
A man escapes from his asylum back into the world,
the world of waggons and dray horses,

of carrion birds and potters
burning in the fog of the marshes.
He escapes where the language no longer

incarcerates him in paper, where words
are only the wood, the church bell
tinning across cut fields. Such silences

are brief, a cold night in a hay cart,
before morning returns him to the prison
that exists and does not, that holds

and cannot keep, whose term is not
honorary or volunteer. Clare, your madness
confirms the losses that never were.

Arcanum

> As soon as I see the word arcanum in any
> proposition, I begin to suspect it.
> — Descartes

Like Hegel's cows, chewing in the final dark
of reason, a domestic passion lies within
the *salus* of a language. Writing

is a privacy. I seal up that child of silence;
it turns its blank, dull face
to the world, and names a proper name.

On that adequate screen, the overcast sky,
what alphabets are traced? Scratchings
of trees, miserable spirals of chased birds,

homely parallels of planes. A writing
that seizes its own erasure, altering
the world it vanishes from. So

the homely alphabet: presence within distance,
ignorant messenger. Writing cannot
comprehend the lineaments of message.

Deaf to its own urgings, it outraces
presence, arriving before beginning,
always already the father of itself.

And the child of a silence, a feminine blank
that is famine and plenitude. Inscription
defaces the black monument of the word,

carving into an originary emptiness
an awful geography, after which all boundaries
are known, all geologies discovered,

all nature transcribed, though its landmarks
face outward, blind to the world.
The features name and are not named.

The Angels among the Liars

Under trees where crows breed
despite what they have heard,
all nature observes the error

of the lying down of angels and men.
Even disreputable angels have a taste
for the human. Theirs is a mating

with the object of their disaffection,
for what impure angel otherwise
could power the air with longing?

What are the intermediacies of the body
but glazes, heavy and crazed?
And what is form but a contraption

of spirit? The forms asleep
beneath the withered fruit
are injunctions of a dusty surface.

Other men sleep well, knowing
there are no angels, and no words
that real or false will call them down.

Money and Dürer

Our heedless statesmen here lose their heads
    and from their silent mouths
admissions flourish, trusting in such a one,
    taking *e pluribus* such another:

How unprepared, the rich,
like the gray knight in "Ritter, Tod, and Teufel,"
    facing obstacles other
than his handbook described, expecting
    the press of metal
on his back and belly, the spear clothed in fur,
    to intimidate the Devil and Death:
Ignoring them, he hopes to fall upon some small
    valley where dragons are mortal,
spear aslant shoulder, far from the walls
    buckling their cables:
He finds long days where a hostage sun hauls color
    from the barns of the dead:
The shattered stalls, the stringy cows
    remain too earthly symbols
of heavenly complacency: His warhorse nibbles
    hay at his feet:
He dreams valleys where the dead die and work off
    the debt of dying,
always with other, poorer valleys to slave in,
    deeper into the famished
alleys of death: He wakes to empty plains:

The stars are needles, the fields sharp with grain:
    Meteors prick the seamless sky:
Now bare lanterns light the lurcher home,
    where money
sleeps outside the houses of the poor,
    cool unreasonable planets
turning one face to the viewer, like love.

Black Harbor

Love denies the precincts of its will.
Though August's busy windstorm swarms
the air of sheltered harbors, brooding harm
against the anchors of the day,
there is no number inked against the kill
that rusts the standing grain. A small hawk swerves
to claw the sparrow its alchemy deserves
and burning windows light the gravel way.
Through season, season, while miners hammer
needles into veins of cannel coal,
the rabbit crawls exhausted to its hole
and dying bees lie mired in the comb.
The crippled hand derides the fetid summer.
The grass absorbs philosophies of bone.

Summer Island

We leave the farmland for the formless coast,
where broken wreaths of breakers trouble
the luckless gull. Past the driftwood litter,
seals loll and bathers sag toward water.

Our landlocked cottage lifts its eaves
above the brassy bay. To and from
the dumpy port, a shuttling mailship
cheats the tides. The damaged lighthouse winks

and aims its eye over the rolling horizon,
where time shuffles its hour
and land settles seaward.
Odd seasons the locked plates shake

the bearings of the hills and grease
the granite monuments. We cannot wait
for nature's declaration of the breach
that bonds the island to the land. A scarred

seawall carves the current back to shore.
Light swings crazily on the corrugated wake.
Back and forth the peeling buoys twist
like targets. Tomorrow we will separate.

Blue Yacht

No opening line ruptures the surface
of silence better than any other.
Already the work has been accomplished
by the brave title. Farewell, title,

now receding into the impoverished memory.
Interjections and farewells
accomplish little toward sinking a well
through the thick, impermeable rock-face

of silence toward—toward what? Not memory
or passion. Or possession. Toward another,
less agreeable silence, the underside of title,
the dolmen marking the limit of accomplishment,

beyond which is *terra incognita*. Accomplishment
for its own sake is odious. The well
or sane do it for money or title,
the nobility or wealth beneath the surface

of feeling. One man is never as good as another.
None of us will last long in memory.
Similarly, no line lasts long. Like emory
board, the abrasive accomplishment

soon effaces the claims of other,
older events. More aggressive lines soon dwell
vividly on the capricious surface
of memory. Take our forgotten title,

doddering into the past like Lear. Similar titles,
other bad beginnings confuse the memory
until that title, that small ship at the surface,
is as forgotten as air to the accomplished

diver. Here the weight of lines swells
the brain as it compresses the body. Other
lines, constantly piling up, smother
the raptured memory. What was the title?

Not even the darting fish remember it well.
What was projected as a silly exercise in memory
is now a *fait accompli*.
We have ended what began at the surface.

Travel

Sir, to find an answer
is not easy among the nervous mass.
Draw near the exile, note his fingers

manicured in pavilions, and the feet
in soft shoes shod. Often from lands
he departs in vanity's offices, knowing

the luxury of refusal; yet how easy
to mistake for courage is fear's glance.
The milk-brick walls

call the hotel creatures into form—
the hourly animals, awake at nine,
brunching at pond-side tables on carp:

a vested hippo, an Anglican giraffe,
the neurasthenic elk beneath their veils.
They too recede, with their daring clothes

and ridiculous manners, footnotes
to footnotes in the loose masonry
of scholarship. Where even accidental poise

revives history's architect,
who sees beyond careless wanderings
the emotional clatter of the age?

Fashion alters politics or love:
like the labors of sex, what is lost
is not so much abandoned as converted

at the Bureau de Change, one currency
for another, tawdry bills commemorating
a presidential fool or dowdy queen.

Folly

Something of folly wipes the air
clean of its pretension, a woman
quilting madness into pattern,

whose gold-threaded birds wing the compass rose
around a wounded tree the parliaments
of flowers choke. The mind's

many deliberations issue
into love like muddy swans
breaching the bank for weeds their deep bills

cannot hold. They preen and sip
and otherwise complain their interest.
There is no love among them,

yet the madness clothed comes on again
and we call it love. But not ourselves,
though we word our declarations to our care.

I've watched three nights
the orb-weavers feast
on the window's steady light, funnel

down which throb the gold-eyed moths
they tangle in their webs and suck.
My face bares back at me

the black behind the glare, while breezes
mock sweet husks of insects spread
within the sticky circle of the dead.

Green Island

By runnels and sea-dipped clover, easing
water out of the headlands, the moon in daylight
scars the severed architecture back to grace.
God the competent, God the antique:

the green island arches
above water's shallow back,
where brine shrimp scatter and the dark
unmannered boats troll. I measure the evil dates

spent staring the same blind channel
toward lumpish heaven. The water swelled
each evening in its grave surround,
the backlit island glowed and was gone.

And what was there, islanders?
Sand dyeing children's rags,
stolen keels athwart tattooed rocks,
beaches soaked with fisher's slaughter,

where gray birds picked the wash for scraps.
What falls away each evening
is not kind authority: the cracked boats adrift,
abandoned swimmers lolling in the crawl,

no green ideal
toward whose curious carvings
one swimmer heads out with broken stroke,
a mote on the horizon, a silent O.

The King of Black Pudding

In the dusty and blood-soaked shop
he could not reason the declining regard
for the blood sausage and Barnsley chop—

hacked from Southdown sheep,
two chops per sheep, the chops
the Prince of Wales could not complete

three years before his abdication.
Albert Hirst did not complain.
A purveyor of pudding must know his station,

but no matrix or linear algebra
could calculate a value for
the caviar of the North, curse of anaemia.

Each morning he swallowed a slice
or two, to qualify his ware.
Though his manner was most precise,

on his ribs reposed a weight
one likes to see on a butcher
or a pig at the slaughterer's gate.

The pigs despite their brooding
cannot serve as pallbearers
for the king of black pudding.

Flour Mites as Moral Beings

Born to a desert, we die in bread,
and if the repetition of our labors
cannot be approved, who, discovering

our secretive gorging, our clumsy
mating in a bed of sand, can condemn
a habitat we cannot alter, knowing

no intimate prospect but whiteness?
Monstrous to others,
we have come to prefer our minute

diffidence, each a stranger to his parents,
as to his children. Who can say
democracy has not given us

an appreciation of loneliness?
All our languages are conjugated in silence,
our etiquette colored by modesty,

our sex legislated by need, never desire.
Can we be condemned because
our philosophers have fouled themselves

with the available, our engineers
narrowed their figures toward
Those-Who-Determine? We accept

the sufficient ignorance of our situation.
We are, at least, masters of dry economy,
not parasites of flesh—and so not

religious—nor like our cousins ruthless
cannibals, uncivilized though hugely beautiful,
with a gladiator's rites and dew-laden nets.

This Island

Strata's dip and strike, reason's rippled sea,
nor any flooded scar prepares
the wreckage of this wandering plain.
Beaches rattle the rusting chain and open

the coiled ammonite, but undergrowth
cannot profane the cottage
fouled by fire, nor the withered apple sprout
palatable leaves. Dingy sheep

the black dogs worry
bleat into their painted wool
while sharp beaks rustle through heather
to hollow eggs. How is their spotted color

the eyes' domain? The keeper
rattles to his boss, and four or five
vacation houses
flame the eastern sky.

Down the cobbled walk,
a body crouches bleeding from its knees.
A hooded man tenders his pistol.
Dry streambeds fill with startled flocks.

from *Sullen Weedy Lakes*

Moorhen

      To have
red mouth and green shanks
      like a sidewalk hooker
come up through the ranks
      of weeds does not disqualify
you from honorary membership
      in the upper class,
the community of spies,
      or any lowly clan
not put off by outer feathers that
      conceal the inward man.

      Or hen in this case, unsexed
like Lady Macbeth or the Chairs;
      though no more rude than the next
species downstream
      you've never grown fat
like a capon on chocolate éclairs.
      The dictionary calls you
a *common* gallinule,
      an insult, I suppose.
Your family has elongated
      webless toes,

      but all families have problems,
marital or genetic,
      in search of a mastering art
or a convenient aesthetic.
      Admiral, it's an admirable life
asleep on the water
      above crepuscular plants
and miniature pike
      that never need to be tended
and never go out on strike.
      You nose among the rank

      roots, washed white and ghostly,
grasses weave on the bank,
      where bugs, I assume, have costly
apartments, and are always behind in the rent.
      And you, you're the rent collector,
dealing in first-born sons
      and daughters, grannies, long-lost cousins,
virtually everyone.
      How convenient to be a ridiculous
rapacious insectivore,
      much better than being dependent

      on a grocery store.
How convenient to maintain a demeanor:
      when chased or thwarted by fear,
you sail between the weeds
      and disappear.
Did you descend from the moors,
      purple and lush with heather,
far away from the stores
      and with indifferent weather?
Better here in the lowlands
      full of *noblesse oblige*—

      where the rats own baby grands,
Inland Revenue never lays siege.
      Reduced to one expression,
call it amused but grave,
      that achieves its own lesson
on the etiquette of where to behave,
      you plod with unwieldy grace
as if the ditch were a minefield
      and not a froth of lace.
I feel estranged
      that way too, sometimes—we all do, hen,

though poor as vole or filthy rich.
    But what use, then?
You'll wake tomorrow and the ditch
    will not have changed.

Capability Brown in the Tropics

Even if evening elected a lover
from countless candidates, the mountain would murmur
against such devices derived from textbooks.
The ordinary architect achieves order
by renting remission to rare fevers,
his plaster walls washed with coral,
a pink imputation, purely informal,
like a greeting to guests, late or unwanted.
His ponds lie open to arrangements of carp,
his muted mathematics nearly a nature
examined by X-ray. Such fish expect no one.
Elsewhere lakes languish, luring to shore
unrepentant anhingas, their oilless wings
spread like the fans of infamous geishas.

The Rivers of England

How we too shoulder arrogance, weapon
of the poor against the poor: our guttering
litanies sung to these arguments.
Gill-netted fish, tubercular badger,

poisoned swan ghosting through bare waters
toward shires flaked of steel and coal.
Asian ports now control the fire before the hob,

the glass toy-theater whose puppets glaze
polished boards. The kestrel's silence, the crow's
triumphal caw, the kingfisher perched above streams,

like a judge over sentences within —

to pluck one out, and make it rhyme with law —
return where water fails to flow from maps:
strikes have hammered shut the rusted taps.

Banana Republics

Gone now, the remarkable harvests
when machete scraped back jungle to reveal
the mossy temple, by next season
frondy undergrowth again. The mothy breathing
of money in foreign capitals, inhaling
its increase, weaves about the paddleboats
sunk at docks, spent mansions
beside the earth-colored river
where a chair floats upside down, its caned back
netting crimson fish threading upstream,
legs rising above the swell
like a snail's waving horns or the drawn swords
on bronze statues of corroded revolutionaries.

Through an open window, night's membrane
rests on a gilt frame where seagulls
turn across a dull oil of sky,
Holsteins browse burnt-umber hills, and the shepherd
swerves his crook against the bready sheep,
loaves for the wolf that slinks against the copse—
or only a sheepdog wronged by veneer—
all to resurrect, above Mozart's snowy slopes,
some species of return where now
the lordly cockroach trembles and stills,
overseeing its domain. A night bird cries.
The lizard on the wall uncurls its tongue
around a fly. The ceiling fan revolves,
a ship propeller turning thickly
through rafts of seaweed; and green moonlight—
as if the moon *were* cheese—immerses the lizard,
the cockroach, the piano in the vast private bay
where marijuana sloops cast off toward customs
of a common shore. Gentle Jorge, late of the bar

in the Hotel de la Revolución, now cradles
his Kalashnikov on a back seat, awaiting the Guardia.
The capitalistic children ask to shine his shoes.

Debora Sleeping

The ferry window frames a pop-art shovel,
jaw drooling gouts of water and harbor mud.
The drawn-in gangplank scrapes against the wood.
A few shy children pelt the boat with gravel,

but the stones fall short. The boat's an oven.
Outside the seagulls circle, lazy and overweight,
crying against decisions of the state
like wingèd burghers stacked up outside heaven.

The French and Spanish ports decline midway
between bureaucracy and art, but while
waiting for the Fifties to return to style
they condescend to watch our nights and days.

You're asleep again, as on the leaf-lit train,
though here a purple plastic chair's your bed.
The pre-Raphaelitic curls that wreathe your head
are permanent—at least, immune to rain,

unlike the satin shirt I made you wear
in Paris, that did not outlast the storm.
You spent the evening huddling to keep warm
and whispered phrase-book curses in my ear.

Sleep's our disease, the heart's adagio.
We wallow in its sty, refuse to leave
the rundown precinct of its raveled sleeve,
the only ease bodies so close can know.

Or so I thought. Watching you here
sleep in hard daylight—hulled on that dream beach,
drugged (courtesy Dramamine), silent, out of reach—
I know the first stirring of a distant fear.

The boat wakes toward chalk cliffs choked by fog,
where fishermen not out of work still bear
the dying and disputed catch ashore.
Dreams are the lover's travel log.

Christ Church, Oxford / 26 October 1881

My dear little girl,

     (There! I don't think I ever began
a letter like that before—in all my life.
     But of course I shall soon have
to alter it: you see our friendship began

     so *awfully* quick—quite dangerous,
it was so sudden—almost like a railway-
     accident: that it's pretty
sure to end off just as suddenly. Next year,

     we shall have got to shaking-hands terms,
and the year after we'll be on bowing terms,
     just when we happen to see
each other at opposite sides of the street.)

     Please do not think I am beginning
to forget you, because I am so lazy
     about writing: but oh! oh!
I'm so *awfully* busy! What with teaching,

     looking over answers to questions,
writing my lecture-business, and these letters,
     sometimes I get *that* confused,
I don't know which is me and which the inkstand.

     Pity me, Marion, my dear child!
The confusion in one's *mind* doesn't so much
     matter—but when it comes to
putting bread-and-butter, and orange marmalade,

into the *inkstand*, then dipping pens
into *oneself*, and filling *oneself* with ink,
    it is *awfully* horrid!
One of my pupils this term is a negro,

    with a tiny face black as a coal,
and frizzly wool for hair. I have had to keep
    a label on the skuttle,
and a label on him, marked in large letters,

    in black ink, "THIS IS THE COAL-SKUTTLE"
and "THIS IS HIM," so as to know which is which.
    Many thanks to your mother
for her letter, and I'll write to *her* some year.

        Always your loving friend,
            C. L. Dodgson

3-13 September 1752

And what an indulgence is here, for those who
love their pillow to lie down in Peace
on the second of this month and not perhaps
awake till the morning of the fourteenth.
From every autumn there is an absence,
a marriage of need to Georgian necessity,
the walnut table abandoning its leaves
like the oaks theirs.
                      Such compromise
still panels an ardor with royal circumstance,
such partial and implied powers as could not stop
the planets in their orbits to illustrate a dogma.
Cholera among the farmers, the lords
muffled in their chambers, a sudden fall
shortened in its count, to whose advantage
other than the diplomats' do the yoked weeks
cooperate?
               And like unruly hedges, hallowing
the rumpled thrushes on their nests, the year
needs pruning. And like the badger, savaged
in its sett, it shrinks a little to survive.
An act fillets its circumstance; and king and lord
will follow Christ's vicar to a settlement
with Caesar, yanked like a fish from the bloody womb.
The sceptre *that* bent out of true, the deaf
will introduce a motion to implicate the hearing.
Even in minor histories, some days have never
deserved to exist. On Thursday awakens the laborer,
two weeks' wages lost, the sun still in the sky,
all lives whittled by Parliament, the month
collapsed like Hogarth's drunkard, trampling on the flag
embroidered, "Give us our eleven days."

The Underground

I

THE THIRD SECTION, 1854

The hollow light of London, late afternoon,
filters across the main bank's central hall,
the paneled chamber that shadows upward toward
the unwashed skylights of a Moorish dome
where mottled pigeons on autumn evenings flutter,
trapped in smoked glass, descending by thin stages
to alight beside a feverish clerk's accounts,
his ledger of foreign exchange now told and tilled
as city churches toll the landlocked hour.
Beyond brass grilles, by mahogany railings stand
the sallow representatives of *beau monde*,
waiting for bills to clear the manicured fingers
of clerks who turn from signatures to stare
at the slight constructive shudder in the walls,
shivering dust from the breasts of wooden nymphs
and the fruit they lie on, launching chalky powder
down on silk hats, through the vague cones of gaslight
spilled from the beryl shades onto the baizes'
brushed green fields, mocking in their cold reminder
of the partner's blown-glass globe that hurls its flakes
of snowdrift upward from the ground, to settle
carelessly on enameled skaters frozen
in stolen passion on a mirrored lake.
Cigar smoke binds the oak Corinthian pillars,
like wild grapes etched within the weedy precincts
of the Coliseum by the *émigré* engraver,
thumbs stained with nicotine, who peers across
the low spiked wicket toward the senior clerk.
The floury ash sifts down upon his shoulders.
Some milk-faced gentlemen soberly discuss
late news from the Crimea, the fall in stocks.
The clerk still scolds his miserable apprentice,

whose hat that noon, toppled by an errant cane,
scattered the canvas reticule of notes
entrusted there, and on the wind dispensed
old money to the crowd of accident.

II

THE CAKE OF CUSTOM, 1914

And what is mastered by the master's pawn?
A gentleman lifts his silver-headed cane
to probe a shattered window, while blasts of snow
ferret beneath the iron overhang
and drift in ricks across his boots. The knop,
fashioned into a monkey's grinning skull,
warms its long-blunted teeth against his palm.
Down needle alleys echo the screams of pigs.
Leaning upon his cane, he takes the gale
windward between two buildings, his glass eye
hollowed with cold, or memory of cold.
He enters the abattoir, cracking his stick
on the Georgian desk three pigs' heads contemplate.
Their candied faces repay the mirrored glaze
of the walnut burl. Two steaming butchers turn.
One wraps a bloody hand around a beer.
Remember still the sainted name of Morphy.
The gentleman lights a bull's-eye carriage-lamp
and with the cane descends the spiral stairs
curving from view, the broken steps long patched
with scraps of splintered lumber, moist walls lined
with peeling bills of fare, the ornamental
menus of smart society that once
found private entrance to its restaurants.
Unlocking a paneled door, he views at last
the circular ballroom lined with cabinets.

Remember still the sainted name of Morphy,
who strode the checkered squares in moleskin pants.
His lamp sets fire to icy shards of glass
melting at his approach and burns the sconces
tilting the gas lamps from the mirrored walls.
Against the pier glass, heaps of chairs and tables
protrude from rotting sheets, a dusty range
of *papier-mâché* mountains once constructed
for Balkan comedies abandoned till
the hills began their languid avalanche.

III

BALACLAVA C.I.F. LONDON, 1854

O take the dead where merchants cannot find
the sunken graves that would offend, offend.
The roll-top warren of pigeon holes contains
among raw bills of exchange, ripe accounts,
crossed letters wreathed in bindings of red tape,
among all these, two tickets to *Otello*.
From his inside pocket, the *émigré* withdraws
a dog-eared sheaf of folded manuscript.
The clerk accepts it with a condescension
required by the manners of the house,
and if the quill that feathers his right ear
should quiver with a confidential tremor,
his eyes betray no human interest.
The odor of stale perfume wads his nose;
but with a shy conspiring air he bends,
examining the Russian manuscript.
He moves his lips in negligent perusal,
then slides the sheets into a lower drawer,
as if to shield from vagrant observation
the moral opportunities war provides,

the flowers, hothouse fruit, and vintage wine
hoisted along the ships and gaily spread
(*O take the dead far hence, at our expense*)
through officers' low cabins, past-due bills
for war that purges from the country seats
Bentham's utilitarians, who bore the strike
of Preston spinners, Sheffield engineers,
or lack of Miniés, medicine, and tents.
Beneath the gibbet, dear, we walked a year,
then south, south to the cold stewed Indian tea.

IV

ROTHSCHILD'S PIGEONS, 1914

The governments sour like vintages of wine.
A ruined printing press subsides beneath
riggings of dust the gangs of spiders wove,
and in one cabinet the forgeries,
long out of date, tilt in their dusty thousands
the bank notes' copperplate. The revolution
honors our failure in cold masquerade:
the dream of 1848 now stains
the weathered stone of Highgate. Frozen markers
shatter until they slant like tenements,
like the geometric problems of parquet
where here and there a crowbar has removed
the ancient underfloor, the swollen river
bricked up and boarded over, a black canal
threading beneath the ordnance map to flush
the rotting sewers to the Thames. I've traced
its late meanders in the dust, as if
the polished course of history consecrates
those passages it passes by, those streets
that Parliament has blue-penciled or forgotten.

Gone, gone, the railway mania, the alley
where little-go men fingered muddy letters,
the ragged shawls selling their silent lights,
the Creole flower girl, the Irish beggar
wheeling along on his low wooden carriage,
porters in bottle-green coats, the beehive stove
beneath the crown of the dome, and clean-shaven clerks.
All these things seen and unsaid, said and unseen,
the pigeons conned each noon in Finsbury,
a lunch wrapped in a towel to keep it moist,
dead partners hobbling by in breech and stocking,
frost-nipped as grandfathers. The pride that fed
the old dispute about the keys now feeds
new trenches in the north of France; and Christ
whose feet were splayed, or nailed with one forged nail,
now violates the truce of dialects.
And No, No, I've never met, I've never met
The man from Alabammy that I couldn't forget.
The dead go squealing to their muddy graves
like music-hall comedians, or slaves.
The groan of pigs from upstairs orchestrates
the lighting of the lamps. Their mantles play
charades upon the ceiling, smoking corpses
repairing plaster wreaths and gilt medallions
now swept in parapets along the parquet,
greased with the ink of blood. The capuchin
presses its apish nose into the bunch
of splintered grapes that crowns these ornaments.

V

The Standard Assassin, 1854

Shadowed by buildings whose unknown addresses
control in miniature the windward hour,
the church bells visible down the narrow street
ring stoutly to the notes of Wren's design.
Out of his hansom cab the pale young man
knocks country mud from his boots and purchases
a *Standard* from the blind newsboy who thumbs
pence, tuppence, farthings into separate pockets.
Within the deepening shade of brass-knobbed doors,
wrapping his greatcoat over a new pistol
like a waiter laying a napkin on his arm,
the blade strides stiffly to the walnut desk,
then with the *Standard* tips the ink pot over;
and as the starched cashier extends his hand
to stop the welling ink, the thin assassin
peppers him in the eye. A porter shouts.
The *émigré* and senior clerk look up,
and when the first removes his spectacles
a vial of acid is flung into his face.
I plunge into the busy crowd, to rue.
They know me still the same, to rue, to rue.
And his smile was unalter'd, rue, to rue.

VI

Bluebottles, 1914

Blind summers when the flies, so ravenous
they clogged the ink pots at the windowsill,
mated upon the rank air of the Thames,
Parliament closed tall windows to the stench,

abandoning government for country house.
Decay attends decay, in measure of
the rising damp, the fall of soot from plaster.
The river's course work cuts its teeth on mortar,
falling on Roman tiles to the blocked drains.
The gaslight flickered. As I drew the cape
about me twice, the long-expected ghosts
refused to rise. From cabinets I swept
the foreign bank-notes with the simian cane,
clandestine knowledge sickening to the fabric
of an English gentleman, however ancient
or disposed against the kiss of government.
There are no longer any who remember
our dead conspiracies, the Tsar's machine
hurling cold vitriol, an eye blown out
by a spy's defective cartridge, and better lost
than forced to witness every further loss
the tenors of this century have sung,
the English armies wheeling toward the Somme.
The threats of youth are lost in youth, and what
the anarchies of foreign war produced
produces schemes of revolution hung
from a frigate's spars. I've brushed ten thousand rubles
into the flood. I've risen to the stairs
to gather from my friends an unwashed ham.

Racial Prejudice in Imperial Rome

Tamquam scopulum, sic fugias inauditum
atque insolens verbum

Change resolves the landscapes
to the duties of mutual subjection,
gulls beating into the wind,

motionless against hornbeam and ash.
These histories approximate the language of the human
until corruption works upon them,

Livy's strutting Gaul, whooping before the tiny Roman,
dispatched with two short thrusts of the short sword.
The outward arts that inward motions fail

fail the razored dossiers crumpled in cabinets,
the hungers that are not the case, the specimens
some view as training; some, terrain.

Consider the grebe's forgiveness, the mocking
of the gargoyle, each irrigating in stone
the meticulous skeins of conspiracy.

To such redeemers tender no contrivance or control.
The heron walks its shadow, the egret its intents,
and our own abrasive elsewhere avoids

the strange and unfamiliar word like a dangerous reef.
Dead mullet float on the lake like fans,
the lakes like blue fans.

Major Graves

On Wednesday mornings Major Graves would walk
around his island by ten o'clock,
brushing with his cane the hair of the natives
and plucking from bushes a raw sedative.

His descendants could not trace the harsh
tracks of his leather boots in the marsh,
though the precipitous decline in alligators
began in his refrigerator.

Every island has its green
regard for vagaries of scene,
but Major Graves could not be held
to responsibilities of the veldt.

The mating cries of the quadrupeds
echoed in his great bald head,
but the notorious volume on wildlife
by rumor referred to his wife.

The bitterberry provided ink
for tattoos and fermented drink.
Evenings the Major embellished his arms
with monkeys and maps of his farm.

In months without r, the absence of storms
permitted arrival of crates of forms
whose small print the natives took to be seed.
Their exports consisted of weed.

Their priests believed that to burn or freeze
was the manifestation of one disease.
After seven years, they erected a god
shorter than he was broad.

Recalled to Whitehall by the Foreign Office,
the Major contracted a jaundice.
He survived the fever but soon succumbed
to a gross infection of the gums.

His wrought-iron balcony from Savannah
supports a legislature of iguanas,
while ornate lamps perched on cupidons
let the dead with the living look on.

To the Honourable Committee

Though now the act is almost commonplace,
to beg relief from strangers courts disgrace;
but since our scholars, poets, and artistes
must worship galleries instead of priests,
it has the force of moral virtue when
it keeps the breathless arts in oxygen.
Arranged around your table in despair,
the poems can't grind coffee, carve a pear,
or make a hat rack dance like Fred Astaire.
They'll never hammer nails through concrete blocks,
and cannot open combination locks.
Great Fannie Mae has ruled: no banker shall
accept a sonnet as collateral,
and in revenge, perhaps, for which give thanks,
the poet never reads his work in banks.
Rude politicians think it rather funny
a poet has a hard time earning money,
or if he earns a bit, and then relaxes,
the IRS will seize his odes for taxes.
Biographers are wont then to distort
impedimenta of the common sort,
for poets, like their neighbors, cannot pass
for saints or martyrs when they cut the grass.
Though verse be undercooked or overdone,
it is unread by all and bought by none,
and so within the democratic state
a poet has a democratic fate.
Because he asks foundations for largesse
who once to kings had ventured in distress,
the poet may be tempted to complain
and soothe with quarrel his distempered brain,
or play the miser, who having priced his words
reduced his speech by half, and then two-thirds.
In time it may be judged by your committee
the artist's last reserve just masks self-pity,

or that for those compression makes obscure
a weekend on the rack's the only cure.
Most honourable sirs, you must remain
as cold as snow, implacable as rain,
but spend compassionate amounts on those
whose lives were better spent in writing prose.
With your award, I'd ask leave to explore
the rundown harbors of a foreign shore
and for a year there rent a terrace house
unfrequented by *Time* or Mickey Mouse.
Like Novocain, loud supplications numb
a charity as kind as cumbersome.
If scrupulous, the poet will refine
the silence at the end of every line,
and thus, in this as elsewhere, rather throw
his voice toward whisper than fortissimo.
Good sirs, I ask approval of this grant.
With kind regards, your humble applicant.

James at Sixty

That year, forced to purchase a garden of thorn
from the most blatant tradesman in Rye,
he built a wall to protect the half-erased landscape
beyond the wall, planning no sheep-creep or stile

that might let the other world master
the complication of this inmost port.
Days he cycled the salt flats of the Cinque Ports,
searching again for the landscape of Hawthorne,

though now America could never master
the proportions that left his felt cap awry.
The man in knickerbockers crossing a stile
into the laminated sediments of landscape

straddled a country whose landscape
failed industry, failed the sinking port
with the courage of its desolation. Style
twisted into hedgerows, a thorn

sharper than scythes measuring the rye
or gleaners who let lateness be their master.
March is a month when little left to master
bothers the impositions of landscape,

when the retreat to London or Rye
shadows a retreat to an unknown port
whose docks are rotten, gates wound with thorn.
In changing light, the mind composes a style

beyond the earlier vastations of style
not even the adequate idea could master.
If the finger were pricked with thorn,
it would bleed prose into the landscape,

fill every stream with the deep red of port
and rise in the stalks of punctuation like rye.
No solitude, no desire drunk on the wry
hour-by-hour accretions of a style,

dictates to his typist this last report,
whose every silence now welcomes its Master.
Outside, the growling dachshund cannot escape
the rope circling and circling the red hawthorn.

Haddocks' Eyes

We've received the morning post.
Royal Mail has sent a roast.
Let the ten-pound package lie
open to the blue-tailed fly.

Meat can be indifferent
with the best refrigerant
but decays within a week
and will spoil its physique.

Language functions like a sieve,
stealing what it can't forgive;
words of praise are bittersweet,
consolation indiscreet.

Soon the gosling and the goose
will attempt to reproduce
and will pardon dead Parnell's
small affairs in grand hotels.

Politics can't save the clerk
shaken by a chance remark
or console the cows that wait
for the slaughter by the gate,

wait for lovers to disgrace
dinner's intimate embrace
while the lakes of gravy sigh.
Frozen in their boats they lie.

Famine from a satellite
won't disturb the appetite
or condemn the butcher's choice
and the methods he employs.

Diplomats soon learn to curse
border wars they can't rehearse;
generals by night confess
to their love affair with chess;

and the tyrant does his part
for the sale of modern art.
In the poker game he plays,
teach the loser how to raise.

Ambassador of Imperfect Mood

Close-eared specimen of the violent hour,
    species of reproach and vanity
wrapped in the unrepentant cloth
of the ministry of power,
forgive the beetle and the moth
    their reluctant Christianity.

Architect of imperfect lakes
    commanding hope of grander
prospects etched on color plates,
while through weeds the coral snake
slides, your hunger annotates
    the burned plays of Menander.

Sleeping villages will succumb
    to the grave Virgilian
virtues of your passing glance
when its martyrs have become
innocents who embrace romance,
    cold-blooded and reptilian.

from *Vain Empires*

The Secession of Science from Christian Europe

Many a terrible monster made of broune paper

I

ROBERT GROSSESTESTE AND THE ORIGINS OF
EXPERIMENTAL SCIENCE

Greek columns, set narrowly against
      the ruptured surface of the Mediterranean,
correct the armies of the declining sun

      where the infant schools of Oxford lie.
To resign all livings for the one
      deception of the senses, a stubborn bishop

suborns himself to the dignity of the page,
      its ink a gall, its rotted berries coloring
meteors in the human eye and monks

      bending to goatish debaucheries.
What doctrine hides in painted capitals,
      where ancient snakes devour their tales

and each learnèd smudge repairs an age of truth
      with terror? Psalm commentaries couch
their penance in mistranslated passages,

      the glass of wine whose outward surface forms
no inward grace. Gears of the natural world
      turn redemption to revelation, passion to possession

of Western clerks streaming to Constantinople,
      sharpening their pens upon Greek noses.
Take now the advantages of compromise,

   the shattered beaker with its poisoned syrup.
On his blunt thumbnail, a mother-of-pearl shard
   gleams with prophecies against the Pope.

A man has his meat, and also his prey.

 II

Theodicy of the Air-Pump of Robert Boyle

The oranges swell within the Age of Reason.
   Across the rusted screen, pad by silk pad,
the gecko presses claim upon the eye,

   black heart soaking through its papery skin.
New realms invent new torture, new anatomies
   that starve the paper from the settling ink,

the fraught wealth turning butchery to science.
   The status of experiment can change
the psychic fraud to overnight success,

   live acid seeping through the sewer's cast.
So in his oaken barrel Hooke decompressed.
   So Boyle stroked his pigeon's ruffled feathers

and laid it in the pump where turn by turn
   sleek pistons stole the air, while in their chairs
nodding philosophers adjusted their wigs

   and watched the captive pigeon suffocate.
They feasted on a roasted stack of squab,
   like Englishmen eating raw seagulls in their search

for northwest passage to the Chinese silks.
What memory corrodes is not the "art" of knowledge.
The purity of science cannot change

  the common sins of beakers and retorts,
the broken backs of coal fields conjuring up
  thin tubes of ether and glass, dead Merlin's spells

transmuting North Sea oil to Armani's smells.

III

HISTOIRE DES MENTALITÉS

Desire reflects our own translucent eye,
  the white corrupted ball of milky curd
that stares, stares upon shadowed galleries,

  the simple truth, if not the single truth.
A glance cannot repair Goliath's oozing head
  or pull the absent skin, like a slipcover,

over the naked horror of the bronze flayed horse.
  Participation in the divine idea
raises the staining tide beneath the bed,

  drains through rotting casements, down stone steps,
mires the counting room and private court
  where peacocks bicker over a roll of dice.

No one trusts the blank check of the patron,
  his bathrobe some faked thread of tapestry
still moist with indigo. A glass-eyed fly,

   he buzzes around the artist's breathing corpse.
The colors of a conscience cannot mend
   the leaden armature of chiaroscuro:

we cannot see that world in black and white.
   Alas! It's easier to reconcile
our chatter to gilt daubs on plaster walls.

   There's no escape from sensibility.
The shuttered pope at Avignon withdrew
   into the sanctum of his private bath

whose steamy clouds were etched with the will of heaven.

IV

JOSEPH BANKS AND THE BOARD OF LONGITUDE

One might in youth concede to investigate
   such practices of the cod as require the French
to creep within their bark-lined suits

   and split the fish in woolen gloves,
not touching the violet entrails,
   or take ship to observe the transit of Venus,

to crawl along a caterpillar of coast
   where among the fray of moral appetites
vast cabinets might be filled with skins

   as rare as scrolls, and eggs whose translucences
were not inferior to the morning star.
   Bligh suffered for his breadfruit trees,

a nicety not recognized at feasts
 where the tropical Pacific changed to wine
and natives traded frail songbirds wrapped in net

 for the hand-carved crosses of the gods.
These gods take breakfast on the flying fish
 or such idle and unprofitable specimens

as would exempt themselves from human company
 and might enamor the queen who should not *chuse
to encumber herself with the stuffed animals.*

 Against those who in the European disease
would place geometry on distant suns,
 one would rather stand within the homely science

of gears, escapement, of the movement of hands.

v

THE AGE OF BALLROOM DINING

In history's deep thicket, each monster wears
 a mask to hide his face, but the salons
require the formalities of skin

 when dining on the courses of illusion.
They powder their tongues with the gossip
 of war, chronic essay of tragedy:

the amputated limb and punctured eye,
 children gutted in the ditch, great humps
of horses, flies clogging their throats,

    such impersonations of pleasure
as on the stage requite the actor's silence,
    the evening in a candlelit room.

A hunchbacked lawyer rises in argument.
    The hour's contemplations now recruit
the fall of tea leaves from an abandoned jar.

    A maidservant of servants, weeping in the closet,
counts minutes wrung from the mantelpiece
    where Neptune throttles his bronze dolphins

and straddles Time, his slender chariot.
    The flaking mirror wraps gilt faces
to its mordant surface. Like photographs,

    they wake from the dream of ambition.
The sleep of knowledge is long and deep.
    To sleep within the wound of sleep,

they wrap their legs in lace.

VI

THE EMBARRASSMENT OF RICHES

What call you the Townes name
where Alexander the pig was born?

The plastered rooms were left to prostitutes
    whose impure sullen skin, like blotting paper,
was thought to draw away the harmful vapors,

      a process known as drying out the plaster.
Communion with the fragrant and the foul
        called down religion from its cleanliness

and wiped the bleeding hands of Lady Macbeth.
      The city that was once the scar of empire
mounted the frail Venetian chandeliers,

      fringed red and blue like airmail envelopes.
Over the Tuileries, a headless king
        might still repent the pestilential church,

the galumphing walk of hobbled gardeners.
      And there, amid the lettuce of the faith,
the politician of the knife and fork

      arms for the armageddon of roast beef.
Philosophers have gathered in the hall:
        there from the flaking psoriatic vault,

whose plaster once prepared a winter sky
        of constellations skewed from native orders,
a spidery pendulum descends by wire

      and slowly knocks against the empty bottles
rayed in a circle, now crossing the chalked mark
        dividing ours from theirs, and theirs from nothing.

They drink the vintage wine from stolen cups.

VII

CHAMBER MUSIC

    The world of physical objects cannot stain
the minor texts our summer nights applaud:
        the firefly's careless shimmer, its Morse code
        of syntax correcting Keats's ode
"To Autumn"'s now tubercular refrain:
There is no mercy where there is no God.

    When Dachau's Jews and whores were sacrificed
to Christian sacraments, no Savior dawned
        like a black sun on the Black Sea: the wine
        of old communion kept the dead in line.
    The weak fish grappled in the claws of Christ,
the osprey turning from His shattered pond.

    We have our music too. It substitutes
the flames of Wagner for the string quartet.
        The violinist cocks his bow, and with a nod
        the bald conductor lifts the hand of God
    and dips his black baton. A barren flute
takes quavers from the rage of sunset.

Christ among the Moneychangers, 1929

Among shivering bankers the coin went false,
and on damp walls the shreds of tapestry
repented the cost of flowers under glass,
the foul pool swollen with fish, small vanities
whose scales were weighed out coolly in silk thread.
The stink of plaster corrupts the polychrome
and carp convert in secret to the cause
of wall-eyed ancestors flaking under crests
now mangy lions rise rampant to protect,
their hair shirts still acrawl with louse and worm.
The raggled matrix of an hour's peace
cannot reform crude factions of a state
never alone except among the mad,
who on their knees vomited up bright blood
that splashed like taxes on the flagstones.
Sumptuous deaths in the shade of politics,
and then the posthumous careers, the charter bus,
the cure of hunting hawks and not their masters.

The Long Vacations

The honeysuckle raged
upon mossy gardens,
sweetness sickening, beckoning
each time we turned a page

of those musty novels by Scott.
The papery moths thwacked
against a hurricane lamp
even the hurricane forgot.

A nameless lady sold us eggs
from her splay-foot, rickety table
with its tempting pool of change.
Her bantams pecked at our legs

but gave up double yolks
Mother fried for her lunch.
Our tomcat stalked the gulls
while she told dirty jokes.

We were, quite frequently, bored
little children, nasty and cross.
After we left they tried,
for murder, a man we adored.

It's difficult to forget, or forgive
the tedious years in a place.
Someone lives there still.
Someone more sensitive,

perhaps. But who forgave
our childish demands?
Out of eight long summers
there's little left to save.

Why, ancient Mary Sowle
who died just a year ago!
She could squeak the exact squeak
of a Baltimore oriole.

A Version of Pastoral

The undersecretary,
mindful of the sharks,
trails across the lawn
in August's purple darks.

He bears a tray of juleps
with mint fresh from the tins
that circle our white houses,
attracted by our sins.

His wife sings "Rock of Ages,"
emptying the pitcher,
then swings it back and forth
like an acolyte his censer.

The undersecretary
assumes a priestly air
and sprinkles benediction
upon our wicker chairs.

He cuts his little finger
on a carving knife.
I am, he reassures us,
Resurrection and the life,

and measures out the cheese
to fit a slab of bread.
By spring the lane of elms
will be a line of dead.

The crickets in the bindweed
chirp like broken pipes.
Stiffly we sit to pose
for a late daguerreotype,

but darkness now has stolen
the light we need to see
the lines upon our faces
and guilts of property.

We laugh and lift our silver
cups to drink a toast
to sweet Kentucky bourbon,
God, and Emily Post.

The Advent of Common Law in Littoral Pursuits

I

From marshy ditch to ruined copse

to ruined corpse, trained arguments confuse
police with politesse. What shy, cadaverous wreck
has understood the season's misconstruals?
Through the stripped thatch of hedges, harvesters

in white linens root their crops,
but in their horsehair wigs confute
the language of the innocent or mute.
The man who murders on his neighbor's beach

murders his neighbor, but on his bloody sands
claims due right of salvage. The islanders
inhabit an island of regard, correction of an appetite,

and take their lesson from the flight of cranes.
They feed their sea of hunger to the flames.

II

The oyster's genuflection in the dark
consoles the season's conscience to the grave

denial working past the hour of dawn.
Dark fishermen thread the fish, or fugitive,
home to the fire, while broken buoys cork
the Irish channel, and migrant birds have flown.
A spray of salt slows the rotting crab;

the coil of seaweed snares a lady's purse,
feathering the sand with the gull's brief surprise,
the magistrate of matchstick ribs.

Along the shelf, the shattered hulls would mock

the salmon muscling upstream to its source.
Like tourists, the broad dunes of October walk
the cloven slate stones and the men-of-war.

Florida Pest Control

The blonde unlocks
her daddy's Firebird,
blood-red as a tropical fish.
Privilege, that old *bête noire*,

shakes its head in her exhaust.
Her rear lights swim
in a fantail's glide.
The South exists,

I write my liberal friends,
with its wage slaves
and Burger King estates
in burning, frivolous pastels.

No one can dream it away,
though plasma centers drain
the blood of black and white,
our ball and chain.

The houses turn to dust
beneath us, gnawed by termite,
beetle, or the fear of God.
Only the past can't be exterminated.

Down the street, Christo's men
sheathe a house in red plastic
and pump three days of poison in.
Last year two hapless thieves

broke a lock and wandered through
a termite-ridden house in Tallahassee.
They choked to death
in twenty minutes. Christ!

The Shadow-Line

A shadow loon flies from the glassy lake
over mangroves and the freshwater pond
where a lone canoeist casts between the fronds
lying along the shore like broken rakes.

He shatters the inky lacquer where the stars
are scattered like a pinch of cooking salt
in the old recipes. It's no one's fault.
The red dot on the tree line must be Mars,

or just a radio tower blinking, blinking
messages two lovers might overlook.
Night fish are rising to the maggoty hook.
I can't tell any longer what you are thinking.

The shadow of the loon will soon embrace
the shallows of the continental shelf
as night becomes a shadow of itself.
Another shadow passes over your face.

We used to spend summer nights listening to jazz—
rude subtleties of the horn! Now we discuss
surrendering to what will happen to us,
or ought to, or perhaps already has.

Van Gogh in the Pulpit

London, 1876.
                    I am a stranger on earth,
hide not Thy commandments from me.
                                    The pigeons swoon
in volleys round the brick Wesleyan spire.
There is soot, the understanding of soot,
along the vision of the Richmond Road.
The terraces move
                        uphill toward grace,
toward the salvation of the ordinary.
And if we look back,
                    back into our disgrace,
from which we have made our little progress,
the gray clouds
                are rent chalky and scarlet,
like the vestments of the Anglican priest.
The working poor of London live as miners
wrapped in black,
                    black-faced along the face of walls
at which they chip,
                  chip with leaden hammers.
The gas will flare and scour the streets
here in the heavenly city.

                          Our feet shall be sockless
and we shall cut our shirts from dry sacking.
We shall be in our normal condition,
                        abasement
before the potato eaters
                    black as loam, kneeling
to the soiled foot of the sower,
bending to the harrowed cloth of the reaper,
the broken meat that fleshes the digger's fork.
Expelled from Paradise,
                    that shall be our paradise.

Britain without Baedeker

I

From the shell's contrary run and the gull's

sugary distemper, the river cannot cover
the metalled road that like a wedding band
binds the island causeway to dry land.
The frost-flecked salt grass taints the winter light:

its slow refusal of the vacant nests
turns toward the marshes like a rough caress
the idea that all of love is property
and property is merely appetite.
The starving birds along the Backs have begged

raw gobbets from the coughing tourist's leg,

and through their mouths the icy figures burn.
Beyond the fen the dead elms queue for spring,
which follows our cold fever with saws and fire.

II

The dunnock and reed warbler brood the lone
survivor whose gross beak outgrows his home
till summer breaks the cuckold from his word

and spreads the voices: drifting, brutal, absurd.

Tristes Tropiques

The nuance of the palm trees
        abuses the regret
of careworn Romeo
        and his fat Juliet
who have outgrown their teenage
        suicide pacts.
Death comes turning the page
        and death is just the facts.

We lose our moral beauty,
        grow sensitive to smells.
The gift shoppe's jewelry boxes
        are glazed with broken shells.
A blood-stained mattress dries
        in the Vacancy Motel.
Life is no version of living.
        Life is just hell.

At night the tourists gather
        beneath the winter moon.
It has a bad complexion.
        It will be waning soon.
Learning how to die
        is finally just an art,
says the shopping mall
        to the shopping cart.

The Burning Man

    At length he comforted the criminal
town councillor or priest, more often women,
        caught in the flytrap of the Renaissance,

the rack's *Malleus Maleficarum*
        on whose thick slats the marriage vows were spat
to heresy's familiars, nine dead cats

    hung drooling from a wooden altarpiece
to mock the crucifixion of our Lord.
        And neither water nor a cooling cloth

was he allowed for their relief, knowing
        the word of God afflicts the innocent
no less than white-hot bars applied by grace

    to heal the lying tongue, the perjured eye,
or drive the seven crippled demons from
        the weakened anus or the vaginal tract.

Two hundred in two years, conducted to
        the final mercy of the brush and stake,
the youngest under nine, a pair of sisters

    who clung to one another in the flames,
a blinded girl whose trembling hand he took,
        and others too numerous or dead to name

or afterwards recall as other than
        a half-charred face, a cage of blackened bone,
both those who on the rack confessed their sins

    and those who still protested innocence,
since none could suffer such exquisite hurt
        without the devil's bland conspiracy.

Their screams reminded him of childbirth,
      their pleas for death that rose to nightmare shrieks
as their dresses caught and drifted up in crumbs

      of glowing ash. More terrible than these,
the laughter of the crowd that warmed its hands
      and later pissed upon the glaring coals,

the stink of burning hair, the incomplete
      cremation of the flesh, which hung in strips
across the smoking corpse like ribbons of beef

      suspended from the crossbars of the smokehouse.
The scent of roasting women was a rare perfume
      to noses cottoned by the stench of shit

flowing through gutters, or the fragrant worm
      that danced from rotting flesh and took its lease
in pages of corrupt Gregorian chants.

      Happy the corpse, because it is dead;
much happier the tortured, still alive;
      more fortunate than either, the unborn child

who has not heard our names or seen our hands.
      Took solace from the wounded and the sick,
and nursed the suppurations of the plague

      when hand-drawn carts drew off the freshly dead
to shallow lime-pit or the burning trench.
      The fever glowed beneath his whitened skin,

his penitential moans like tallow candles
      melting with plague, the straw bed hot with fleas
that took his last confession, though his tongue

    had swollen like a steer's, his swaddled groin
attained the rank consistency of cheese.
    Despite his protests, argued in the full

Aquinian logic of a Latin doubt
    and published in the double-columned fonts
that like the Wehrmacht wheeled through provinces,

    the murdered would have sentenced him to sit
in the dock of the accused at Nuremberg
    with those who knew but did not dare to speak;

with those who spoke, but did not dare to act;
    with those who might have acted, but did not;
with Auschwitz doctors and the Dachau whore.

Animal Actors on the English Stage after 1642

Now the dog all this while sheds not a tear

Bearwards, ape-leaders, owners of trick horses,
down the long vans from Africa and the north
the stunned survivors of the Inns of Court
in frenzied howls accepted empty purses,

knowing they were guilty of high treason.
Still those who unrepentant had returned
beneath the smoking boughs of lime trees burned
by fleeing royalists, their long hair chastened

seditiously in curls, at these banned houses
in humble standing offered to besiege
their dream within the drama of the stage,
though Cromwell's ass just muttered empty phrases.

A ravaged bear, fresh-baited at pit, staggers
toward the benches howling for Prince Hal,
the monkey shaved in motley plays the Fool,
Macbeth's three bulldogs lick their bloody daggers.

Flower, of Zimbabwe

They dined Thursdays in the Army and Navy Club,
whose porter—it was a House of Commons joke—
was more distinguished than the oldest member.
Two old-school types, one almost cancerous.
The gaunt one lit his old-school pipe, and gazed
into the crystal tumbler of a horse's neck,
then pulled a paper cutting from his pocket.
"His name was Kenneth Flower, damn fine chap—
ran agents from the grass huts of South Africa
through Mozambique, before Mugabe shook
our school chums from their office suites, if not
their suits. Thought nothing of judicious murder,
as casual as slapping a mosquito—
once bribed a bush priest with Afrikaner gold
to ship his students to guerrilla camps,
recruits for Zanu-PF. But there's the rub—
Ken kitted them out in poisoned uniforms.
The chemical pregnation of the cloth
leached slowly through their skin, and in the grass
they stiffened for the vultures, not the Church.
It couldn't last—the deaths seemed damn suspicious.
To tidy up, Ken shot the bloody priest,
who never twigged that Flower was the head
of state security, which bugged his nave
and buggered him in the apse, you might well say.
Guerrillas blamed each other. Flower turned
his coat the day Mugabe was sworn in
and served the blacks with equal diligence.
He had a bit of a giggle, don't you think?"

The fat one nodded, and waved his cigarette:
"You had to know your Ovid in those days."

Keats in India

1848

Just as the sun went down, the monstrous bats,
fatter than crows, with tissue-paper wings,
unloosed their hooks from thick-ribbed, stringy palms
and calmly sailed about us through the dusk.
They pillaged the garden mangoes' lumpy fists,
which tasted like apricots smeared with turpentine.
We'd shut up all the windows to keep cool—
the air was gravelike, but an open door
blazed like a furnace mouth at Colebrook Dale.

Next morning we embarked by the Burning Ghât,
a squalid ground as deep as a London square.
Each cluttered hut of straw and spit, leaning
against a leaning wall of powdery brick,
encased a sickly Hindu like a shell.
Along the water's edge, the funeral pyres,
smoking and sweating, finally exhaust
the little tepees of sticks that families
have gathered there. I saw two bodies burning,
frizzling like cakes and giving off perfume,
the old familiar sweet and fetid stench
that reeked our clothing in dissecting rooms.
Above the walls, the hurgilas comport,
half-stork, half-vulture, stiff and sorrowful
as village mourners. Call them adjutants—
they pose as motionless as marble statues
until their meals are cooked. The carcasses,
like fresh-baked bread, steam in the morning air
and when the wood has sputtered out are pitched
upon the tide, floating in misery
back to the shore, or blindly setting sail
along the sacred Ganges to the sea.

The hurgilas flap out, perch awkwardly
upon their breasts, and tear the roasted flesh.
The sick who still procrastinate their death
are dragged down to the river, where relatives
fill up their open mouths with sacred mud.

We had engaged a frayed Bengali pinnace
of sixteen oars, decked over with bamboo,
the low, light fabrication of our cabin
just slashed bamboo and straw, a rumpled cottage
without a chimney, much less a chimney pot.
The boatmen crouched above us on a grate,
fretting the water with their bamboo oars,
long stalks tacked at the end with rounded boards.
The river flattened like a sheet of paper.
Rice grounds on either side stood glistening,
soft with the calls of white-scarlet paddybirds,
each homely village masked with blossoming fruit,
like scenes of Oxfordshire along the Thames!
The dirt floors of the houses swarmed with frogs
plumper than goslings, speckled green and black.
The boatmen there were towing us with ropes
against the current, limbs and muscled backs
grown scaly from their hourly immersions.
They used to swim aboard like water rats
when porpoise larked about our sluggish passage.
We grounded on an island made of sand,
bordered by reeds and curling grass—ashore,
we came upon the fresh prints of a tiger
prowling beneath a gibbet where two men,
almost reduced to skeletons, were hung
in chains. Its feet were large as dinner plates.

At sandy Sibnibashi we were plagued
by clouds of hideous insects clogging our candles.

Some burned away their wings on the glass shades;
others flew straight into the boiling craters
to meet a waxy death. We paid no heed
to what next day became a ghastly spectacle,
the army that was fluttering on the ceiling
wet with fresh paint, and clung there blackly rotting
until the ants devoured them. These kindly bugs,
my close companions in this airless cabin,
share out the moldy store of my provisions.
As if to save me from my own complaints,
they've eaten up a box of bluish pills.
Some fakirs swam aside to beg for alms;
but one stood on the bank, a raw-boned devil
like Shakespeare's Edgar topped by a filthy turban,
a mad array of rags and wretchedness—
two satchels flung across his narrow shoulders,
the shredded length of a scarlet cummerbund,
a palmetto leaf he held like a lady's fan,
waving it coyly the while he laughed at us.

Old Dacca was the wreck of antique grandeur,
its castles, mosques, and dainty palaces,
the factories and churches of the Dutch
all sinking into ruin, were overgrown
with cobra vines and bushes of the jungul.
The palace court now hosts a tiger hunt—
here we were made unwilling witness to
the practice of suttee. The bamboo stage
is thrown up in a morning, crudely roped,
the body then prepared in state upon it.
The widow is led out and stretched beneath,
entombed in brush or twiggy combustibles—
they have to drug the younger girls with wine.
Pressed down with long bamboos, she starts to cry

as they drench her dress in ghee. It flares like resin
when the solemn relatives ignite the stage.
Her whining screams are terrible to hear.

We came to a drowning country, cheerless marsh
and seas of reeds, but briskly on we sailed
like a greyhound through a field of broken corn.
Bull alligators glide about our boat,
lifting their long black snouts in friendliness,
except a monster, fifteen feet in length,
striped black and yellow like a garden wasp.
We passed a drove of swimming cows, the herdsman
towing himself by their hips and hairy tails,
guiding the Judas beast with a broken staff.
A smartly bangled, hennaed country woman
came quietly down to bathe at Mongyr Ghât.
She stepped in with her mantle wrapped about her,
with decency and seemly modesty,
and as the river stirred beyond her breast
she squatted underneath—so long I thought
nothing could save her. And only then she rose
and strode like a goddess up the dusty path.
The distant Greeks, I almost am convinced,
long followed similar custom. How otherwise
could clinging pleats of sodden drapery
have charmed—or hypnotized!—the Old World sculptor?
Later that day we saw a murderer.
One of the sailors, bathing by himself,
spied through the reeds a fakir strangle a man
and bury him in the sands. We passed the spot
and watched the demon wash the blood-stained clothes;
but we were far from the authorities,
who doubtless would have taken little notice.
The Thuggees, who we thought had been suppressed,

are said to promise to their goddess Kali
an offering of lives, like English tithes.
We might have shot him with impunity.

We landed in Benares, holy city—
the Chunar sandstone, polished with coarse rags,
is smeared with deep-red paint, then populated
with elephants, with gods and goddesses,
with women, men, white bulls, and flowerpots!
The sacred brutes of Siva, tame as mastiffs,
walk sleepily up and down the narrow streets,
and lying down can hardly be kicked up.
There is a stinking, templed monkey-garden,
blessed by the ape who conquered old Ceylon—
its denizens are fat and ripely orange.
They creep out to the fruiterers and dine
impertinently on the wares, or snatch
rich gobs from the mouths of children at their meals.
An Englishman was drowned last year in the Ganges
for having shot a beast in ignorance.
We saw a few examples of the penance
where holy men distort their arms or legs
by posing them for years in one position,
or clench their hands until the curling nails
grow out the backs. We saw a dancing cow.
The astronomical observatory,
thought ancient and now crumbling into ruin,
still has a course of lectures. Prim young men
in spectacles, fast sweating through their suits,
produced a roughly painted plaster globe
and waved their hands beneath the southern pole,
where they suppose the sacred tortoise squats.
And this a Government establishment!
They showed the sun sail gaily round the Earth
as if they lived in Alexandria

and I were Ptolemy. Pilgrims descend
the pink stone steps, where thousands of both sexes
are occupied in bathing, where merchants hawk
their wares beneath the shade of gay umbrellas.
These pilgrims buy two pots, called kedgerees,
and, tying themselves between them, paddle out
to the center of the stream, sit bobbing there,
then tip the pots until they fill with water
and sink into eternities of rest.
I wish that Christian death were thus obliging
and sold the pots that promised our salvation.

We now proceeded overland by horse,
our servants armed with spears and hammered swords.
The camels followed like a caravan!
The country from Allahabad is jungul,
uncultivated, flat and wild, broken
by marsh, impassable in rain. Poor Wordsworth,
I think, would button up his collar and huff
at all these casual miles, no walk in sight,
and scarce a bush of which to make a poem.
We have to wrap our heads in turban cloth
while our bearers try to whistle up a wind,
like English sailors. The sun has blistered us,
though dawns are freezing cold, and the shade chills.
My servant is insensible to weather—
he sleeps all night on the gharry's open roof
while we catch shivers in the smoky carriage.
One eve I dragged a blanket up to him
and asked next morn whether it gave him comfort.
"Oh, very, sir," said he. "It was my pillow."
Half down a bank, there lay an elephant,
groaning, groaning, a mountain of flesh and bone.
We gave the wretched animal a cordial,
but all the bearers could not hoist it upright.

It haunted me the long slow miles to Lucknow.
At last the iron bridge across the Goomtee
rusted before us. Our horses steamed and snuffled,
clacking their iron shoes. The muddy river
ran sullenly below; and on its banks
a few white figures worked with sticks, stirring
the dusty smell of India — like barley!
Across the river, there were the domes of Lucknow,
like gems within a chalk of dazzling white,
the buildings knocking one against another
down miles of riverbank, and each one more
majestic, airy, stranger than his neighbor,
while scores of minarets, pale spiky needles
taller than Nelson's column, pierced the dry air
with a twisting, frightening grace not of this world.
Each burning dome was crowned with burnished gold.
I stopped the horse and leaned against the view —
the glare of Indian sun shimmered about us.
The ground itself became a polished mirror.
There was the dream, the dream of fairyland.
At last, I thought, at last I have been taken
into the Orient's magnificence.

We rode like princes through India's mirage;
but, as we rode, the vision thinned and wavered.
The distant, starry color of the buildings,
serene Italian marble in the sun,
up close was whitewash, fly-blown, peeling like skin.
The marbled walls proved only stuccoed brick;
and the gilt domes, the perfect draftsman's arcs
as massy as St. Paul's, were shells of wood
in many places rotten, roosts for doves
that murmured, murmured, flaring in dusty clouds.
You come at last to the conclusion,
the city of your dreams is but a fraud.

For half a mile, we threaded narrow streets,
the filthy lanes between the crowded houses,
crossing the wreck of a handsome avenue
broader than Oxford High Street, with Gothic buildings
that same pale oyster—I might never have left.
The mazes opened into a paved square
with a large and dingy, now deserted palace
used as a market, and there amid the trash
an elephantine gateway, Room-ee-Durwazu,
the most complacent arch I'd ever seen.
Room-ee-Durwazu, called the Gate of Rome,
by which these strangers mean Byzantium.
Like Alexander, there I was at last,
come continents to face the long road home.
I have begun the "Ode to Darkness" now.

from *Night Battle*

Florida in January

The cold of winter is somehow colder here,
the trees bleaker, with their rags of Spanish moss,
the very air clipped and impatient.
You wouldn't realize summer's forest,
so much like New England, grew in a mattress of marsh,
until the leaves were down. Beneath the second growth,
a low fringe of starved palmettos
fans out in short, childlike arcs, their palest greens
worn almost to the color of old dollar-bills.
In rye fields and feed lots,
amid the swaying, wheezing cattle
lost to their mute philosophies,
stalk our self-important tourists, the sandhill cranes—
Nature's aristocrats, eyes flared with red eye-shadow
(carelessly applied, as if without a mirror),
their jaunty icepick heads eager or greedy,
but their bodies delicately boned as young ballerinas.
They high-step away in virginal unease.

Nothing repairs the indifference of their gaze,
neither the storm casting its tattered cloak
over the sand pines, nor egrets huddled
against the lake's border, folded up like origami paper,
nor the water, sullen, pocked and greasy,
a rusting tintype of our latent democratic vistas.
Like Ovid on the Black Sea, the restless stranger
might feel such cruel beauty monotonous.
But, inshore, a crusty alligator steams,
nosing into reeds to let off passengers
or take on canvas sacks of mail,
as if the weather had never once been tender
or required, like love, a moment of surrender.

Sundays in the South

The gravid gecko lies
aslant a stalk of banana,
just a tilde over
the n in *mañana*,

translucent as a thin
slice of kiwi fruit,
with two small beads—
or seeds!—for eyes. The root

of all evil is motion,
its body seems to say.
A crab spider looks it over
as it overlooks prey.

With a pebbly rattle,
tubercular pigeons sun
on the hot tin roof,
the roof of Sin,

burning, burning
over those fierce Christians
sinning—or singing, perhaps,
much louder than sinning.

The pigeons roost in judgment,
mottled, maculate angels,
complacent but nervous
above the stacked cannonballs.

Heat is a form of love,
boasts the courthouse square
to the Frank Lloyd Wright
air conditioner.

Fruit bats lodged in the eaves
shadow the low gas-fire
of sunset, whose bankrupt palms
open their broken armatures

like Edwardian ladies
at the season's last tea-dance—
black fans, black fans!
And, at a distance,

thunder, a great steamroller,
rumbles now with a sad consent
over the tropics' grandeur
and diminishment.

Mother on the St. Johns

The palms looked wary in broad afternoon,
thin women in fancy ribbed hats.
Beyond them the hooded sweep of the St. Johns

gathered home the overweight mariners,
yachting caps askew as the afternoon broke up
and boats shuddered to the bank.

Indoors, beside your chaise longue, cigarettes
were burning mad, their heads alight.
You lit them one after another,

as if you could torture them all.
The condo's wide-screen TV blocked your view.
All life was now a miniseries;

and the Florida sky, that long brocaded curtain,
was about to be drawn over the closing night,
where a thorny, ungrateful gator

wallowed on the shared ledge of bank,
home, or willing to call it home,
the incoherent kingdom. And then a heron took off,

beating its wings like a broken angel,
neck crooked backward in a childlike Z.
Its arc hesitated above the palms.

Darker, but not so injured now.

from Long Island Sins

I

SEDUCTIONS OF THE SWIMMING CLUB

The working mothers never worked aloud,
those afternoons spent poolside, lean and tanned
amid the apparitions of the crowd.
The petals of their suits were caked with sand.
No black face ever troubled their repose.
At sunset, servants in white uniforms
showered the greasy dust off with a hose
as summer broke the dark in lightning storms.
We drank in the politeness like a sin;
each deferential sir, each honeyed ma'am
reminded us that powers ranged above us.
Our mothers drank martinis and sweet gin—
we were too young for anyone to love us.
That fall our boys invaded Vietnam.

III

After a Line by F. Scott Fitzgerald

Southampton, Hot Springs, and Tuxedo Park:
lost in the backwash of the Crash, the War,
the refugees of grace were washed ashore.
The girls who once were "miffed" or "truly vexed"
would soon acquire the morals of a shark,
waltzing the railroad barons round the floor,
their cold, triumphant necks a jewelry store.
And in the shadows the next drink, and the next.
Where does it go, the moment of desire?
Lost, rattling down the Special's corridor,
the distant vein of lights in semaphore;

lost, the champagne glasses tossed against the fire,
the bullet laid inside a lower drawer.
And there is love, cruel love, the last to bore.

Blues for Penelope

The roses are gone, and the hollyhocks,
but still each night I mend your cotton socks.
Now our little boy's got the chicken pox.
Ulysses, honey, when you coming home?

The boys hanging 'round mean nothing to me.
Two from Trinidad. One from Tallahassee.
I don't need more boys to stir my sugar tea.
Ulysses, honey, when you coming home?

All night I'm waiting by the telephone.
I haven't paid the bill and I'm all alone.
Don't you never hear those voices in the dial tone?
Ulysses, honey, when you coming home?

Life without you is a heart attack.
You grabbed your suitcase and started to pack.
I know you'll roll up in a brand-new Cadillac.
Ulysses, honey, when you coming home?

You're a man who couldn't cross the ocean
without making a scene or some sort of commotion.
Out in the sun, you'd forget your suntan lotion.
Ulysses, honey, when you coming home?

I'm tired of living on welfare checks.
Jack Daniel's straight is better than sex.
Now they tell me you left no forwarding address.
Ulysses, honey, when you coming home?

Last night I had the strangest vision.
Two big bay horses had a collision,
and there was your face on the television.
Ulysses, honey, when you coming home?

Nothing

Below us the gray fields of England
lie like sacks of cement
as I fill out the landing card
of Her Majesty's government.

A girl adrift under her Walkman
is sipping her father's *vin blanc*.
I turn to study the orange juice
and a new moon of stale croissant,

our "continental" breakfast.
I've paid with a handful of dimes
for the vodka spilled at my feet
on the crumpled *New York Times*.

A pale silver wrinkling, or kneading,
on the green Naugahyde of sea
disturbs the aluminum cowl
of the engine by GE,

and a coarse white whisker of ship
blinks in simple Morse code
the danger of scotch on the rocks
or ice on wet strings of road

across the stubble of Dartmoor
where black pools on western slopes
surround broken needles of light
that might be needles of hope.

We are tired, bloodless figures,
the waxworks of Madame Tussaud.
How little we really expect.
How less than little we know.

The bowmen who nocked their arrows
on the fields of Agincourt
protected these gas storage-tanks,
the docks of this tiny port,

the small rural railway-station,
the zipper of British Rail,
the consolation of life
built on HO scale,

the silver sigh of a river
squeezed from a tube of paint,
the chalky scar of high street
and a crossroads that stares like a saint.

I remember your dying, your anger,
alone in a hospital bed.
The dead help no one living
and the living no one dead.

In minutes we will be landing
at the airport of status quo.
We never escape very far
from the deaths that await us below.

The English Light

Above the slate roofs, Turner's blinding light,
the light of the atom bomb,
glowed like a car cigarette-lighter.

The center was everywhere
and circumference nowhere, like a medieval God—
His triumphal heavens reduced to X-rays.

Two trees soldiered up the hill,
souls of the damned—pitiless, self-assured.
Scars of red poppies

ordered a field of minuscule, deckled cows.
That night we set sail
on the tides of the back garden,

tire ruts burning like St. Elmo.
Something made its way through the mist—
an electric pylon with murder on its minds.

A third presence was always with us.
Our voices steamed the air
like the gossip of cattle.

Larkin

Hull was a rainy country. The damp of suits
slumped on their wooden hangers understairs,
the wet umbrellas dying in the hall.
The ink-stained carpet. The sodden shoes. The hats.
Beneath the street, drains took away the filth.
His head felt like a boiled egg with spectacles.
Each window streaked with rain or after-rain,
the river swollen to the mud-thick roads
gave nothing back. One might as well get on with it.
And in the country, the drowning of the toads.

No one can imagine how the end will go,
lonely companions: the bottle and the lamp,
the naked girls who pose for you alone.
And somewhere distant, the ringing of the phone.

from Paradise Lost

I

THE CITIES OF THE PLAIN

Reduced to skeletons, the cows
cropped the leafless, broken boughs.

As she passed, a crooked frond
muzzled the shallows of a pond.

The arbors hung with rotting grape.
Beneath them lay a sickened ape.

The full moon, torn like an evening gown,
shone its justice on the town.

From the hills, she felt a shiver
as a ferry crossed the river.

On the plain, a cone of fire
tangled up, behind barbed wire.

She realized it was no one's fault.
Now in her mouth the taste of salt.

VI

EDEN IN THE DUSTBOWL

She was her own celestial city now.
The ravens and the crows in residence
were fallen angels of the picket fence.
Behind it stood the Devil's Jersey cow.
Each dawn a cold, forbidding sun still rose.
The dishes were still there to put away,
but something different—well, she couldn't say.
Perhaps it was the closet full of clothes.
How could she know what true confession was?
Two squalling kids, a husband on the make,
and that June evening with the coral snake—
a devil is not paid for what he does.
There, there in the clearing hung the golden bough.
She stood amid the garbage with her sow.

Song

Her nose is like a satellite,
her face a map of France,
her eyebrows like the Pyrenees
crossed by an ambulance.

Her shoulders are like mussel shells,
her breasts nouvelle cuisine,
but underneath her dress she moves
her ass like a stretch limousine.

Her heart is like a cordless phone,
her mouth a microwave,
her voice is like a coat of paint
or a sign by Burma-Shave.

Her feet are like the income tax,
her legs a fire escape,
her eyes are like a video game,
her breath like videotape.

True love must be a physics test
or a novel by Nabokov.
My love is like ward politics
and drinks by Molotov.

For the Hostages

They wanted to sell wheat, spare parts, and weapons.
The Secretary minded his own business.
In Tokyo, he received a cable.
The Colonel's secretary had transposed two words.

It was unseemly to ask a foreign government for money.
The President would be gravely damaged.
The Secretary had deliberately been left in the dark.
If there was a villain, it was the Admiral.

The Secretary had a hazy idea what the real story was.
The men around the President considered him an enemy.
The President was prone to delusions of grandeur.
The Colonel's secretary had transposed two numbers.

The Admiral's days were numbered.
Numbers often reveal more than they intend.
The President sent an unmistakable message.
If there was a spare part, it was the Admiral.

The money was deposited in the wrong account.
In no version is there any hint of an altercation.
The President had not made up the numbers.
The Colonel's secretary had transposed two enemies.

Not until months later was the wheat recovered.
Now the President's wife went into action.
She wanted to end this matter once and for all.
If there was a wrong account, it was the Admiral's.

Not until months later had the press recovered.
The President blamed them for questioning his numbers.
He had learned numbers and forgotten numbers.
The President had made up his mind.

The weapons did not come without problems.
The spare parts did not come without an enemy.
The wheat did not come without delusions.
The sources did not come without weapons.

The Words

He wrote the words then; they would have to do.
He hadn't known the words had been forbidden,
or that in other hands they were not new
He couldn't see just what in them was hidden,

or why his fathers had been paid to speak
a language whose intentions all were planned.
The withered storks who cried in ancient Greek
would never know their meanings had been banned.

The cunning of his verbs was not mistaken,
the gaze of his dry adjectives not flawed.
But when he tried to show just what he'd meant,

they claimed his meanings were an accident,
and every guilty subtlety a fraud.
The words once put to sleep would not awaken.

Dear AC

I lifted the tea tray over the slanting lawn
in Grantchester's withered apple-orchard,
crusts of your sandwich gathering

a mock empire of ants, black ships swanning
the uncharted distance to Japan.
Cambridge was a closed city,

its gardens unkempt pathworks (I mean *patchworks*)
of ivy behind high walls. Here and there
a rotted gate, a broken slatted door,

gave onto a view of the ordered life.
The vision of roses, the philosophical
dented watering can, even the laboring bees,

not Marx's but Bentham's,
took their liberties within their lies.
I could never be religious again.

What lingered in *New* England that last morning,
as dawn carried the frost off shard by shard,
away from the cardinal with the battered wing

who feathered, ghostlike, and began to sing—
or creak, really? Over your bed, no feather of fan
drifted down, as if from pity,

no owl kept watch, no arguing meadowlark.
The air you breathed was not the air.
There was your red dress on the floor,

there the fruit and the greasy knife,
there your stones, your broken shells,
there your *Sonnets from the Portuguese*

(awful book). There the grieving telegrams.
What are poets without their lives?
Are they less poetic then?

for Amy Clampitt (1920–1994)

Dear DD

The paperboy arrived, the afternoon
of your first byline
in the *Boston Evening Transcript*,
and into the yard rattled your dapper fiancé,

the Quaker Oats salesman
in his company car.
You put the paper aside. The photographs
of that other world, so near to us

in black and white.
Eighty years have put the city in the country,
the pruned gardens out of date
as whalebone corsets.

Your grandfather, a packet captain
on the North River, young captain of captains,
was salt-preserved and famous as far as Fall River.
And then your parents,

impossibly aged, black-worsted beetles
emerging with canes from their forties Packard.
In the attic, their tilting piles of unread *Time*.
Here Barbie and Gampie,

brand-new as cellophane, lie in your shoebox,
her tea shop and his grocery,
all that life we could wish for them,
then wish for ourselves.

Old and then young again, old then young,
like a fairy tale. Beneath the last curling Kodaks,
William at Humarock, emperor of castles
swept by the next tide.

Or *is* it me?
As you lay on your deathbed,
plastic tubes through your nose,
your daughter my mother could not rouse you.

Your eyes had that thousand-yard stare.
"It's William," I said. "William, the poet."
Your eyes cleared,
and then, in a hoarse, hunted whisper,

"You   only   think   you   are."

for Dorothy Drew Damon (1900–1994)

My Father as Madame Butterfly

The dark blue stain across the river
staggers under the lightning.
The radio plays Puccini.
He turns back to the mirror with his razor,

my father, holding it like a dowsing rod.
When it comes, he will be ready—
the main chance, the ship coming in.
Happy families are all alike.

That's what they tell the other families.
Out the window, the little town is rousing,
a flock of grackles
blacking the sky like construction paper.

The boxlike milk-truck chuffs up the street.
Fishing boats have hauled anchor
at Lee's Wharf. Beneath the floating dock,
rare petals of algae bloom.

There above our bunk beds, trophies,
the swords of swordfish,
blunted, bony, a curdlike gray.
The thrash and curl of battles underwater:

a Dürer woodcut on the plain of blood,
men tramped underfoot by armed horse
or pierced by lowly footman's pike.
A petal of blood

curves across my father's cheek—
he's nicked an old scar.
Was that *Superman* we were reading,
or *Man and Superman*?

for W. Donald Logan, Jr. (1925–1990)

Pera Palas

Up. Up. The greasy cables creaked,
raising the polished cage of mahogany
through the marble stairway to the clouds.

The clouds were Turkish, frothy, cracked,
Tiepolo's angelic hangers-on just pigeons now,
veering shadows across the skylight's filthy glass.

The grand, or grand-no-more, hotel
looked down on the steam-wreathed Golden Horn,
glazing the seven hills of ancient Istanbul.

Atop each kneeling mount, a gray mosque
squatted, its narrow minarets
aimed like Pershing missiles at their god.

Each view not a lie, but the fossil of a lie,
the windows flickered at dusk, recessed ministries
to the low chime, the wing-collared visitors

slung in sedan chairs past gathered boats,
like diplomats nestled for concession,
past the steaming locomotive and the nut seller.

We inherit but never inhabit the past,
blistered pieties betrayed by a word,
winched in the *deus ex machina* to bespattered heaven.

Alexander Sarcophagus

Heaven, like most heavens, was built for followers,
not the iconoclast or stiff-necked heretic
but the time-serving, kowtowing companion to gods.

The killer dawns that Alexander faced,
each horizon fresh-stocked with enemies,
left smoking cities behind, steaming litter of corpses,

a backwash of retired sergeants made king.
The past juddered in the dark like a sculptor's mallet,
rose in the royal necropolis, where the last kings of Sidon

were consigned to flesh-eating stone.
The stone had a life before it devoured a life,
before the worked borders of egg and tongue,

drilled scroll of grapevine, the doll-like figures at hunt:
now the panther learning the edge of the axe,
now a Persian kneeling—then a knife in the neck.

The blood tide washed across the steppes
until the moon of Alexander was stopped by a virus,
red lance frozen to his scarred hand. The stone

turned naked stone again, even the good laid to rest
where the past has no need for forgiveness
and the future no need to pardon.

www.ingramcontent.com/pod-product-compliance
Lightning Source LLC
Chambersburg PA
CBHW031136090426
42738CB00008B/1103